MOMENTS THAT DISAPPEAR
CHILDREN LIVING WITH EPILEPSY

DON'T
TURN
AWAY

For a free color catalog describing Gareth Stevens' list of high-quality books, call 1-800-341-3569 (USA) or 1-800-461-9120 (Canada).

Don't Turn Away
Meeting the Challenge: Children Living with Diabetes
Moments that Disappear: Children Living with Epilepsy
Going Places: Children Living with Cerebral Palsy
Finding a Common Language: Children Living with Deafness
One Day at a Time: Children Living with Leukemia
Seeing in Special Ways: Children Living with Blindness
We Laugh, We Love, We Cry: Children Living with Mental Retardation
On Our Own Terms: Children Living with Physical Disabilities

Library of Congress Cataloging-in-Publication Data

Bergman, Thomas, 1947-
    Moments that disappear: children living with epilepsy / Thomas Bergman. —North American ed.
        p. cm. — (Don't turn away)
    Includes bibliographical references and index.
    Summary: Describes the medical problems and daily routine of a twelve-year-old Swedish boy with epilepsy.
    ISBN 0-8368-0739-1
    1. Epilepsy in children—juvenile literature. [1. epilepsy. 2. Bergman, Joakim.] I. Title. II. Series: Bergman, Thomas, 1947- Don't turn away.
    RJ496.E6B47   1992
    618.92'853—dc20   91-50335

North American edition first published in 1992 by

Gareth Stevens Publishing
1555 North RiverCenter Drive, Suite 201
Milwaukee, Wisconsin 53212, USA

Editors: Amy Bauman and Valerie Weber
Series designer: Kate Kriege
Layout designer: Kristi Ludwig

Printed in the United States of America

MOMENTS THAT DISAPPEAR

CHILDREN LIVING WITH EPILEPSY

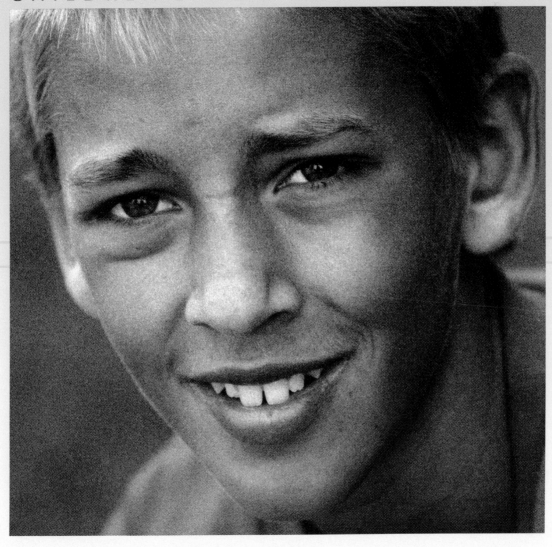

DON'T
TURN
AWAY

Thomas Bergman

Gareth Stevens Publishing
MILWAUKEE

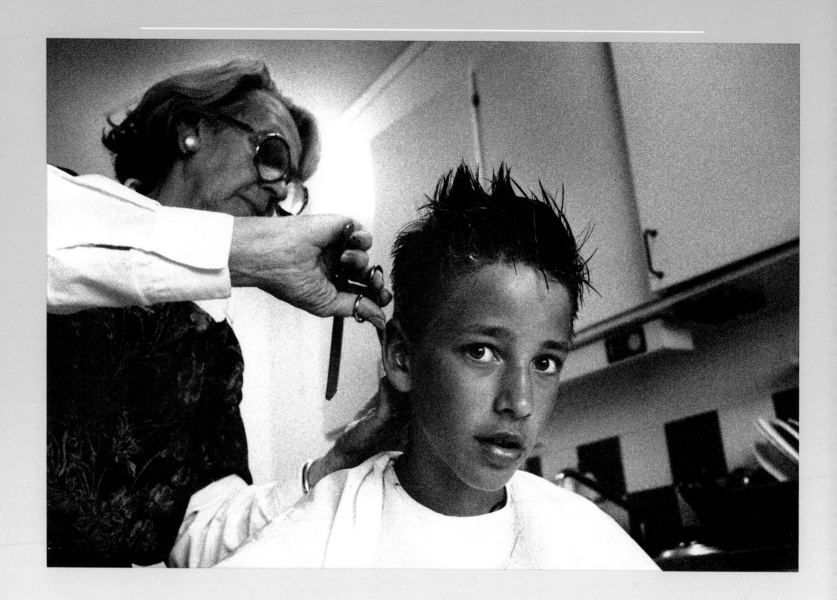

*T*he Don't Turn Away series concerns children with many different kinds of disabilities and illnesses — mental retardation, cerebral palsy, blindness, physical disabilities, leukemia — all lovingly photographed by Thomas Bergman, Sweden's best-known photographer. But it is one thing to share, however briefly, in the lives of other parents' children and quite another to see our own children confront a disability. So I greatly admire Thomas's courage in documenting his son Joakim's discovery of and struggle with epilepsy. I also applaud Joakim's openness in allowing his father to take these remarkable and intimate pictures.

When we see Thomas's striking black-and-white photographs and read the insightful text, we may begin to understand how children and their families face this medical condition. Because epilepsy is a "hidden" condition, not immediately visible, it is easy to misunderstand epilepsy, its symptoms, and what it's like to have epilepsy. Medication and education can help children and adults with epilepsy lead lives that aren't overwhelmed by their medical condition. And, with the help of books like this one, education can also help foster understanding for families and friends living with people with epilepsy and other medical conditions.

I hope you will take the opportunity to learn more about children with disabilities. I hope, too, that you will be moved, as I have been, by the intensity and passion of this man who cares so deeply about children.

Gareth Stevens
PUBLISHER

For over fifteen years, I have been photographing and making books about children, especially children made vulnerable or fragile by special conditions and disabilities. This book is about my twelve-year-old son, Joakim, who has developed epilepsy in the past six months.

Epilepsy is an invisible condition that can limit a person's ability to function. At times, it has been terrifying to Joakim and to us, his parents. Joakim has not completely adjusted to his epilepsy and to the limits that have been imposed on his activities. This may take some time.

In the meantime, it is important that we make decisions that keep Joakim safe but do not limit his activities or freedom too much. Joakim does not always agree with our decisions.

The past six months have brought many changes in Joakim's life. He has had to stop playing basketball and trumpet because of his epilepsy, but he has taken up tennis and keyboard. School has become more difficult for him because of his seizures and fatigue.

In time, Joakim may stop having seizures with or without medication. But seizures are not the only issue that is important to his well-being. It is crucial to Joakim and to other children with epilepsy that people understand what epilepsy is because there are many misconceptions. It is often hard to explain in simple terms what it means. That is why I have written this book.

I am grateful to Joakim for letting me make this book. My warm thanks also go to Dr. Mia Hovmöller at the Children's Clinic at St. Görans Hospital.

Thomas Bergman

Thomas Bergman

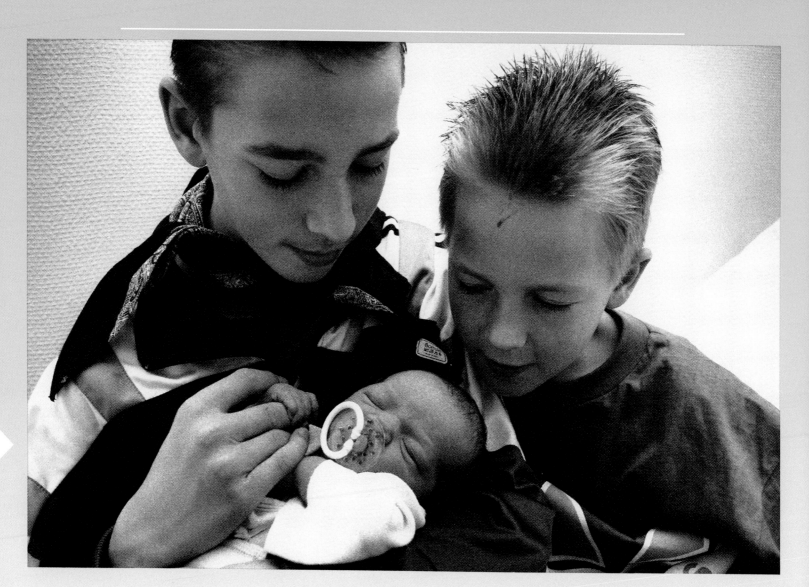

JOAKIM

This is Joakim. He is twelve years old and lives in a suburb of Stockholm, Sweden, with his parents; his younger brother, Sebastian; and his baby sister, Amanda.

Joakim has epilepsy. Epilepsy is caused by a sort of shower of electrical signals in the brain. This shower causes seizures that can take many different forms.

Six months ago, Joakim had his first seizure at home. He lost consciousness, fell to the floor, and had a convulsion. The seizure lasted about five minutes. It was very frightening.

After the seizure, Joakim was taken to the hospital. There, doctors examined his brain with a CAT scan to see if it had been damaged and performed an EEG to measure the electrical activity of his brain.

A few days later, Joakim had his second seizure, which was just like the first. The doctor prescribed medicine designed to prevent any more. Joakim had to stay in the hospital to allow doctors to study the effects of the medicine. His parents stayed with him, too. After two weeks, the doctors felt they had discovered what kind of epilepsy Joakim had, and he was allowed to go home. But it was still a month before Joakim could go back to school.

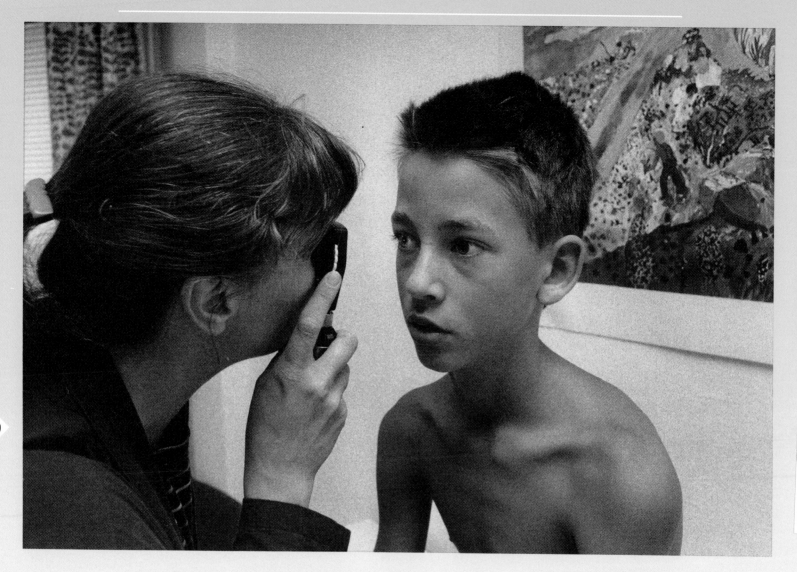

Today, Joakim has an appointment with his doctor. He calls her Mia. She has studied Joakim's latest tests, and she asks him how he's doing. Joakim tells her that he hasn't been doing very well. He explains that he often has absence seizures that cause him to lose track of what is going on around him.

Mia listens to what Joakim is telling her, and they talk a little more about his friends and school and the problems his absence seizures are causing. Then she examines him, listening to his heart and lungs, checking the reflexes of his arms, hands, and feet, and shining a light deep into his eyes.

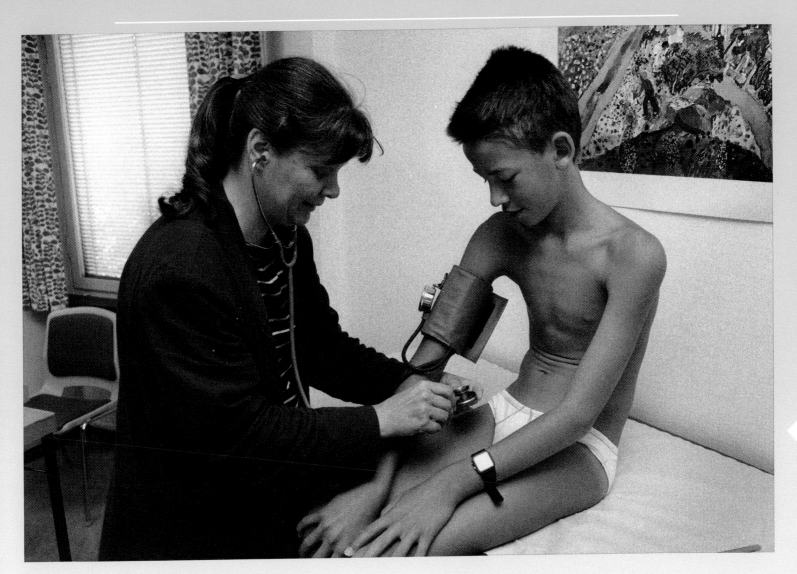

Mia tells Joakim to take a few deep breaths. When he does, she notices that he has an absence seizure. He doesn't fall, but he stares straight ahead. Joakim doesn't hear or see anything around him for a few seconds.

Mia tells Joakim and his parents that he will start taking a new medicine to control the absence seizures. The seizures that caused the convulsions are gone now because of the medicine he is already taking. But before starting the new medicine, she wants to do some more tests.

Joakim likes Mia. She often calls to talk to him about how he is doing. That means a lot to him and to his parents.

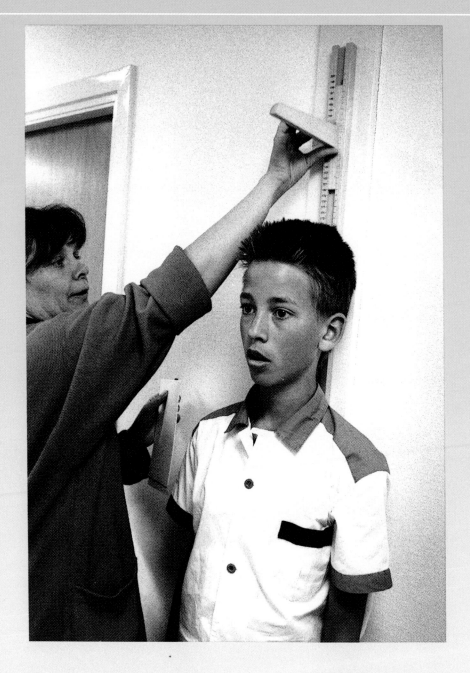

Mia weighs and measures Joakim. He has grown very tall and thin. After she has finished her examination, she explains about the blood tests that he will be taking. The tests show many things, including the amount of medicine that is in Joakim's body. The medicine must be precisely measured so that it is enough to prevent seizures, but not enough to cause other problems. Joakim prefers having the blood sample taken from his finger. When he stayed in the hospital, the nurses took blood from the crook of his arm every hour to check his medication levels.

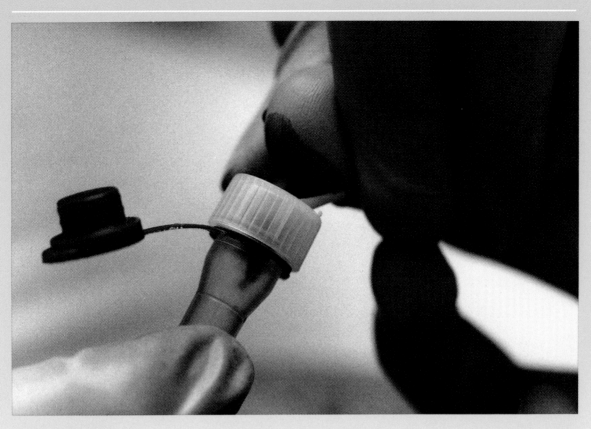

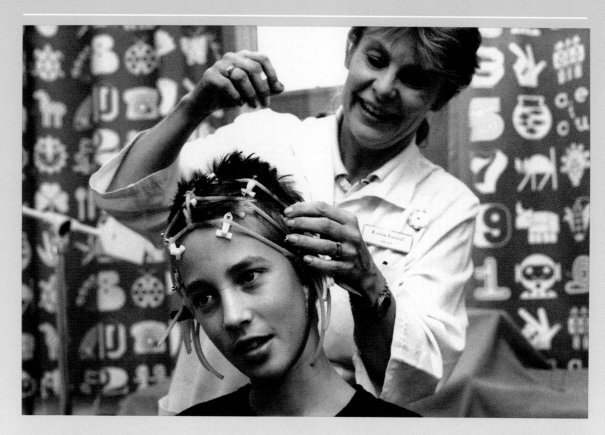

14

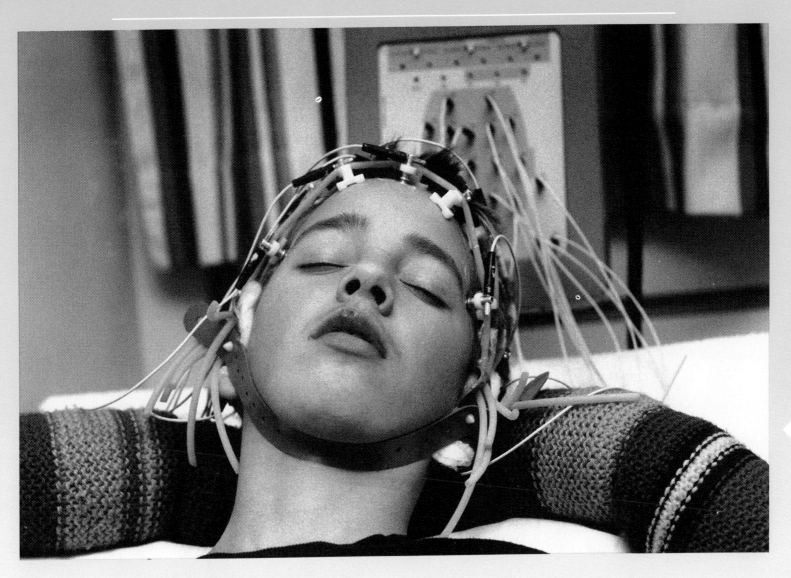

Joakim has had an EEG, or electroencephalogram, exam before so he knows all about it. The nurse, Karin, puts a system of rubber cords that fits like a cap on Joakim's head. Then she fastens twenty small metal cords and plates to the cap. These cords send signals from Joakim's brain to a machine that draws the waves the signals send on a long piece of paper.

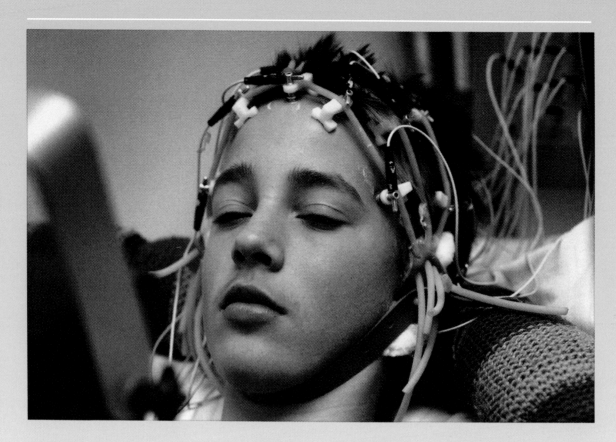

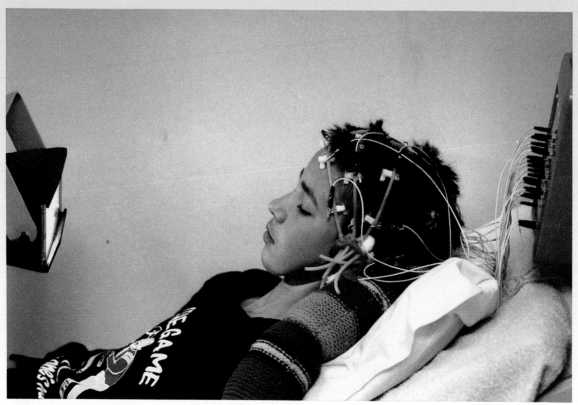

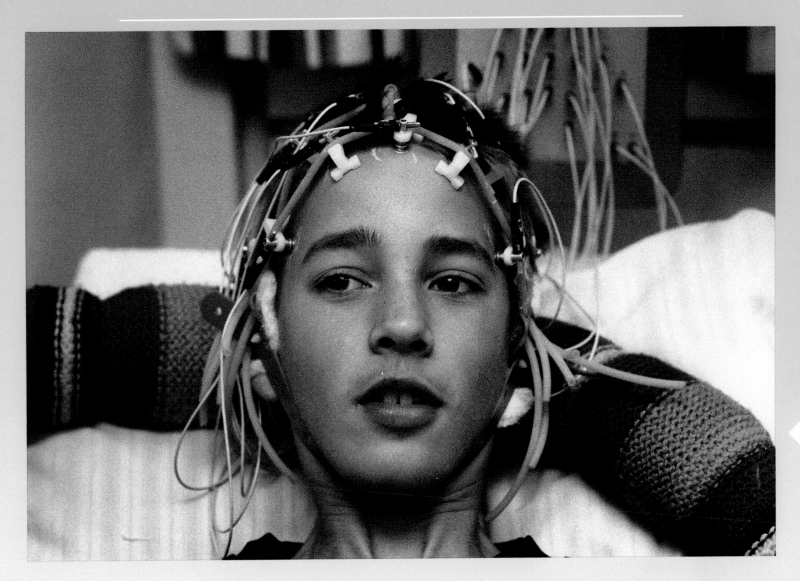

Joakim lies still and opens and closes his eyes when Karin tells him to. Next, she tells him to breathe deeply for three minutes while she watches the marks that the machine makes. Finally, Karin holds a lamp in front of him that gives off flashes of light, some bright and some dim. The last time Joakim took this part of the test, he got a bad headache, and the flashes of light caused absence seizures. This time, though, nothing happens. Later, when the doctor studies Joakim's EEG, she sees that there were disturbances in his brain patterns only when he was breathing deeply.

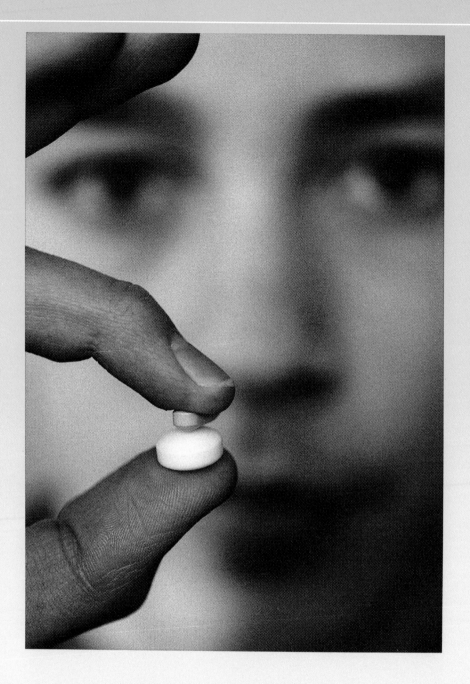

Every day, Joakim has to take two different kinds of pills to control his seizures. To make this easier, he has a pill dispenser that holds enough pills for a week. The pills for the morning are on the left side, and the ones for the evening are on the right. With the pill dispenser, Joakim can tell if he has forgotten to take his medicine. This has happened.

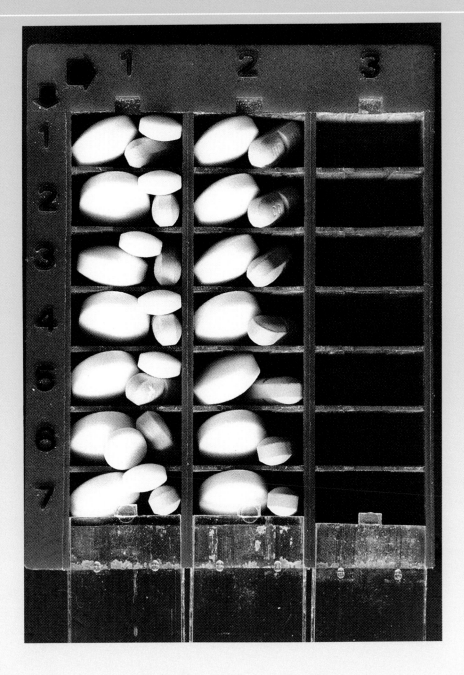

At first, the medicine made Joakim very tired, and he often got headaches and felt too sick to go to school full-time. But he still wanted to take the medicine because having seizures was a lot worse. Now, Joakim is feeling better most of the time and can go to most of his classes. Still, sometimes he is too tired in the mornings to go to school.

Joakim calls his friends Mathias and Peter to see if they can go jogging. They live in the same apartment building, so within minutes, everyone is suited up and ready for fun. The boys jog to a nearby wood and then to a track where they can run and climb obstacles. The track also has a tall climbing tower, but Joakim knows he cannot climb it because he might fall if he has a seizure.

Joakim, Peter, and Mathias stay at the track all afternoon, running, climbing, and jumping. They take a break with the lemonade and donuts they've brought with them before they jog back home.

Sometimes Joakim remembers the seizures that signaled the beginning of his epilepsy. The first time, he fell head first in the bathroom and hit his head on the wall. The second time, he fell off his chair while he was doing his homework. In the hospital, he once had a seizure just as he was waking up. Each time, Joakim became unconscious and had convulsions. When he awoke, he could not remember anything that had happened.

He used to wonder if he could die during a seizure. He felt he had to be careful all the time, and in the beginning, he was afraid to go out alone.

Now he wonders if he will be able to drive a car when he gets old enough. His doctor has told him that it is too early to answer that question. If he is no longer having seizures when he is old enough for a license, he may be able to drive. But it will depend on what the laws are where he lives.

It is still early in the course of Joakim's epilepsy. Many questions will have to be answered later.

It's summer, Joakim's favorite season of the year. The family has more free time, and they can all go swimming. Joakim loves the long, sunny days when he can sunbathe and build sand castles. But he is not allowed to go swimming by himself, and that is very hard for him to accept. Joakim thinks he'll be just fine, and sometimes he rushes into the sea without telling anyone. But he never knows in advance when he will have a seizure. And if it happens when he is alone, he might drown.

Joakim would like to go to a public pool with his friends to swim and dive from the diving board. His parents only allow him to go if he is with other adults whom they know and trust. But they won't let him use the diving board because he might get hurt if he has a seizure when climbing the ladder or jumping. Joakim really wants to dive, and this rule makes him both sad and angry.

Before Joakim developed epilepsy, he was doing very well in school. But after missing nearly two months of classes, he fell behind. With help from one teacher twice a week, he has pretty well caught up. For added help with math, he also meets his teacher, Mr. Hardy, at home on one Saturday a month. After studying for a few hours, Mr. Hardy makes them a snack, and they take a break.

Mr. Hardy has traveled all over the world, most recently to Saudi Arabia. He shows Joakim an outfit he bought there and lets him try it on.

Both Joakim and Mr. Hardy enjoy these Saturdays. They've become quite good friends.

Joakim has much more trouble getting started in the morning than he did before his epilepsy started. He is often very tired when he wakes up, and he sometimes has absence seizures. He says his head feels "twinkly" and very heavy. The seizures only last a few seconds, but they leave him exhausted. He needs to lie down and rest for half an hour, and sometimes longer. Then he feels well enough to go to school.

If Joakim's day is long and he gets home late, if he feels too much pressure, or if someone upsets him, Joakim sometimes has absence seizures. Having a seizure always disappoints him and makes him angry. Telling his mother or father how he feels usually helps lift his spirits.

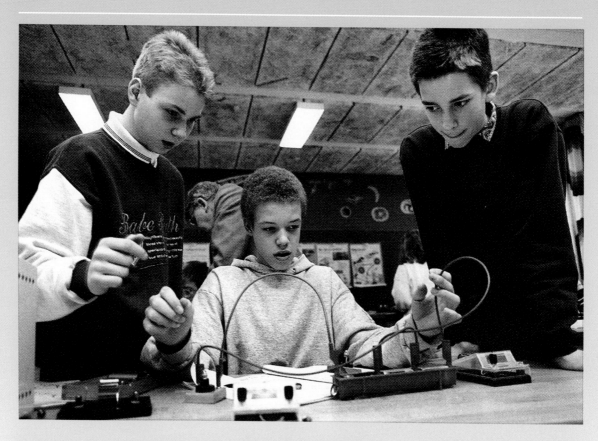

Joakim's favorite class in school is physics. Today, he has lab. He and two other boys are working together on an experiment. When they finish, they will record their results in their notebooks. Next week, they will have a test on what the experiment showed.

After physics, Joakim hurries to his locker to get books for his next class. The school day is long, but it passes quickly.

Joakim is a serious and hardworking student. He is used to getting good grades. But these absence seizures cause him trouble. They are very short and nearly unnoticeable to people who aren't looking for them. But they break off his concentration right in the middle of a sentence or a thought. And, because they leave him so tired, they affect what comes afterward for some time. This can be bad during a test or when he's trying to learn something new. Unfortunately, some of his teachers and fellow students don't seem to understand.

Joakim's mother, Kristina, usually keeps him company while he does his homework. They have lively talks about all sorts of things to break up the work. Joakim needs a lot of help and encouragement because the medicine makes him tired and affects his concentration and memory. He is not happy that it takes him so much longer to do his work than it did before he had epilepsy.

When Sebastian gets home from school, he wants to play an electric hockey game with Joakim. Joakim is glad for the break, and the game is fun and noisy. Sebastian and Joakim often play together, and sometimes they fight because they both hate to lose. But they make up fast so they can play some more.

I am Thomas, Joakim's father. I work as a photographer and a writer.
Here, Joakim and I are sitting at my light box, studying photo negatives.
Later, I will make prints of the negatives we choose.

I've always taken pictures of my children, but when Joakim first developed
epilepsy, he did not want me to take any of him. He just wanted me to be
his father, not his photographer.

Later, though, Joakim asked me if I would make a book about him. He had gotten more used to having epilepsy and didn't mind me taking pictures anymore. He studies my pictures carefully to see if he likes them. If he doesn't, he tells me.

It was a wonderful day for Joakim when his sister, Amanda, was born. He considers her his special gift, and he bought her a tiny white teddy bear with his own money.

Sometimes at noon, he rushes home from school to see Amanda. He carries her around and plays with her until both of them are laughing and chatting in Amanda's baby language. But Joakim still doesn't change diapers.

Today after supper, Joakim's grandmother comes to visit. She used to be a hairdresser, and she usually cuts Joakim's hair. But today, she's just stopped over to bring him a magazine that he always reads to keep up on the music scene.

Joakim used to be on a basketball team where he once won the award for being the most valuable player. But after he developed epilepsy, the team and the coach had to go ahead without Joakim until his medication levels were adjusted. Unfortunately, Joakim lost his place on the team. He was hurt by this because basketball had been so important to him.

Now, Joakim and Sebastian take tennis lessons. Joakim wants to be able to compete, but first he has to learn the basic game. After their training session, the boys sit down with the coach and talk about what they need to work on before their next lesson. Joakim is not surprised to hear that he has to practice his serve.

Music makes Joakim happy. He loves to sing and listen to tapes and records. He used to belong to a choir and was getting quite good on the trumpet. He had to quit playing trumpet when he got epilepsy because he got dizzy and his head ached when he played.

Joakim has a new instrument, though — a keyboard that he got for Christmas. He can already play a few popular songs from sheet music, and he likes the keyboard as much as he liked trumpet. He practices every day so he can get back into the music school where he studied trumpet — this time playing keyboard.

Joakim's doctor tells him that if he goes three years without a seizure, he might not have to take his medicine any more. Joakim clings to this hope and believes that he will be free of his epilepsy when he grows up.

QUESTIONS FROM CHILDREN ABOUT EPILEPSY

*W*e're all curious about someone who is a little different from most of the people around us or someone who may have a disability. Sometimes if we can ask questions and get satisfying answers, we become more comfortable with those people. Here are some answers to questions children (and adults) often have about epilepsy.

What is epilepsy?

Almost everybody knows something about epilepsy, but even today, most of what they know is probably wrong. So maybe it's best to start here by saying, first of all, what epilepsy is *not*. It is not insanity, it is not contagious, it does not cause death or brain damage, and people with epilepsy are not a danger to themselves or to others.

So then, back to the question, what is epilepsy? Most simply, it is a condition that results from a sudden, temporary change in how the brain works. Normally, the brain cells and the other cells of the body communicate through a system of electrical signals. If the electrical system goes awry, it sends more electrical energy to parts of the brain than normal. This electrical overload causes what we call an epileptic seizure.

What happens to people when their brain pattern is interrupted?

Many things can happen depending on what part of the brain is affected. If the whole brain receives the extra energy, it results in a generalized seizure. One type of generalized seizure causes a convulsion where the person falls to the ground, unconscious and stiff. A fall is sometimes followed by jerky movements of the arms and legs and a loss of bowel and bladder control before the person regains consciousness. Another kind of generalized seizure causes a person to stare for a few seconds and then return to consciousness. This is very common in young children who may not even know it is happening.

Seizures also result when only parts of the brain receive the extra energy. These are called partial seizures. What happens in a partial seizure depends on the part of the brain that is affected. Some people hear strange sounds or see things that are not there because their hearing or sight center is affected for a short time. Others may repeat certain actions for a short time, such as adjusting their clothes or walking in circles. They seem to be conscious, but they really do not realize what is happening for the moment. When the seizure ends, they will not remember their activity. Other people black out or become confused for a minute or so. Others simply stare straight ahead for a few moments and know what is happening but cannot take part in it. Some people report strong feelings of fear or other bad feelings for a few seconds. Others say that it is like having someone flip through the channels of their memory too fast.

Most seizures don't last more than a few minutes. Many last only a few seconds. But they usually leave a person feeling confused and exhausted. Some people, however, will not know they have had a seizure and will feel fine immediately afterward. People's experiences with seizures are very different from one another.

What makes the seizure happen?

In most cases, no one knows why the electrical system of the brain goes awry at the time that it does. For some people with epilepsy, a flickering TV set can cause a seizure, while for others, sleepless nights can bring one on the next day. Some find that their seizures always occur in bright sunlight. Generally though, trying to figure out what causes seizures reveals no helpful answers.

Does having a convulsion always mean that a person has epilepsy?

Not necessarily. Young children sometimes have

convulsions when they have a high fever. Adults can have seizures if they suddenly stop abusing drugs or alcohol, or if the fluid or chemical makeup of their body is disturbed. One convulsion does not mean a person has epilepsy — although he or she should see a doctor because it does mean something is wrong.

How does a person get epilepsy?
In about two-thirds of the cases, doctors do not know what causes a person's epilepsy. In about one-third, they do. Of this one-third, nearly half of the cases of epilepsy are caused by damage to the baby's brain before birth or at the time of birth. Other causes are serious illness during childhood, head injuries, and brain tumors. Sometimes the epilepsy occurs shortly after the event that causes it, but often it does not occur until years later.

Can epilepsy be prevented?
Most epilepsy cannot be prevented, but some of it can. The brain is the control center of the human body and needs to be protected from damage both before and after birth. Here are some things that cause brain damage, including epilepsy, while the baby is still inside its mother: poor nutrition, infections, drug and alcohol abuse, physical injury to the mother, and injuries caused by a difficult birth. It is important for these and other reasons that women have quality medical care when they are pregnant.

After a baby is born, automobile and bicycle accidents, diseases, and rough treatment are major causes of brain injury. Young children should ride in infant seats whenever they travel in a car. They should wear helmets when they ride bikes, especially in traffic. Measles is a preventable disease that can cause brain damage. Children should be immunized against measles and other diseases. And of course, babies and children should never be shaken or hit, especially in the face or head.

What are the signs that someone has epilepsy?
A person who has a convulsion should certainly check out the possibility of epilepsy with a doctor. But without a convulsion, the signs of epilepsy are less easy to detect, although it is just as important to recognize them. Here are some things to look for:
- Periods of confusion or fear
- Blackouts
- Staring
- Periods when a person seems not to hear or see what is going on, although he or she does not fall unconscious
- Uncontrolled jerking of legs or arms
- Sudden strange tastes, sights, or sounds
- Repeated activities or movements.

Epilepsy should be considered if a child is having trouble following what is going on in school. If the child is having short seizures that nobody notices, she or he may be missing bits of what the teacher is saying. If this happens often enough, the child will have difficulty understanding directions because he or she has missed at least part of the instructions.

How can a doctor tell if someone has epilepsy?
A combination of hearing about a person's symptoms, tests, and observation helps doctors determine if a person has epilepsy. At the beginning of treatment, the doctor will ask several questions to help a person recall signs of seizure activity. If the patient is a very young child, this information will come from the parents, but older children themselves will be able to supply much of what the doctor needs to know.

The doctor may also ask the patient if he or she felt anything unusual before the seizure, such as a cool breeze or a strong sense of fear. These are called auras and often come before a seizure. The presence of an aura will help tell the doctor that this is probably epilepsy and not something else.

43

Besides listening to what the patient tells them, doctors will do tests. The main test is an electro-encephalogram, or EEG. This test measures the electrical activity of the brain and prints the measurements on paper. The doctor will also examine the person very carefully, looking deeply into the eyes and observing reflexes and movements that might show brain injury.

Can epilepsy be cured?

Nothing doctors can do can cure epilepsy, but it can go away by itself, especially when it starts early in a person's life. Over two million people in North America have epilepsy. More than 100,000 people are newly diagnosed each year, and one-fourth of them are children.

How is epilepsy treated?

The most common and effective treatment for epilepsy is medication. There are several medicines that doctors prescribe depending on the type of seizure and the location of the source of the seizure activity in the brain. Some people have more than one source of activity or type of seizure, and a combination of medicines may work well for them.

The use of medicine to eliminate or limit seizures has made it possible for millions of people with epilepsy to lead normal lives. They hold jobs, drive cars, marry, have children, and take part in professional sports. For some, taking medicine means they may have seizures rarely or never again.

For others, the medicine is not as effective. In these cases, surgery may be helpful if the source of the problem can be clearly indicated and corrected without damaging other parts of the brain. Surgery is becoming more of an option now that techniques have become more precise and less damaging to the surrounding tissues.

Other more experimental methods are being tried that work in a few cases. Their applications may not be wide, but when they succeed it's worth it. Biofeedback, a technique that teaches people to control their body's activities, and a high fat diet can work for some people. However, these are very demanding routines.

Can epilepsy cause other problems for people?

The main problem people with epilepsy have is dealing with the prejudice and ignorance of others. Through the years, people with epilepsy have been considered magical, evil, insane, dangerous, or completely disabled. They have been locked up for life in institutions and prisons, denied the right to marry or have children, barred from schools, and even killed. The treatment has included branding and outrageous medications.

Although the treatment of people with epilepsy has improved greatly in recent times, many of these people are still denied the right to be thought of as independent and competent. This can be very damaging to them.

What kind of life do people with epilepsy lead?

Because epilepsy takes so many forms, it is difficult to make statements that apply to everyone. That's why it is important that people with epilepsy and their doctors be allowed to make the decisions that are best for them. Laws and regulations should not limit what people with epilepsy can do.

Most people with epilepsy make the same kinds of choices about their lives as anyone else. They decide for themselves about college and jobs, sports, marriage and children, where they will live, and what they will do with the rest of their lives. Their epilepsy has little effect on the people who work or go to school with them.

44

FIRST AID GUIDE FOR EPILEPSY

Here are some things you can do if someone near you has an epileptic seizure.

If a person is having a convulsive seizure:

1. Keep calm, and tell others to keep calm, too.
2. Remove any sharp or hard objects from the area, but don't try to limit the person's movements. Just let the seizure run its course.
3. When the person begins to come around, tell him or her that a seizure has occurred but that everything is okay now. Make sure that he or she has a way to get home safely.

If you can possibly do the actions listed above, they will make the person more comfortable. Don't force anything.

You can also:
1. Loosen the person's necktie or collar.
2. Put a flat pillow or folded jacket under the person's head.
3. Turn the person gently on his or her side so that breathing passages are clear.

Don't put anything in the person's mouth. No one is going to choke or swallow his or her tongue.

Call an ambulance if:
1. The seizure lasts more than ten minutes.
2. Another seizure begins.
3. The person does not wake up after the movements have stopped.

If a person is having a non-convulsive seizure:

1. Remain calm, and tell other people what is happening so they don't interfere.
2. Keep the person from further danger.
3. Let the seizure run its course. Don't attempt to restrain the person.
4. When the seizure ends, tell the person what has happened. Make sure he or she has a way to get home safely.

45

MORE BOOKS FOR CHILDREN ABOUT EPILEPSY

Listed below are other books about children with epilepsy. See if you can find them at your local library or bookstore, or ask an adult to order them for you. You'll learn that people with epilepsy are not that different from anyone else.

Dreams Come True. Korfield (Rocky Mountain Children's Press)
Epilepsy. McGowen (Franklin Watts)

Julia, Mungo, and the Earthquake: A Story for Young People About Epilepsy. Pridmore and McGrath (Magination Press)

These publications are available from the Epilepsy Foundation of America at the address given on page 46:

Answers to Your Questions about Epilepsy
Because You Are My Friend
Me and My World Storybook
Seizure Man, First Aid for Seizures
Spider-Man Battles the Myth Monster

PLACES TO WRITE FOR MORE INFORMATION

The people at the organizations below will give you free information about epilepsy if you call or write to them. Tell them the reason for your interest so they can send what will be most useful. You can contact the national organizations listed below, or you can call a chapter of the Epilepsy Foundation near you.

National Institute of Neurological Disorders
    and Strokes
National Institute of Health
US Department of Health and Human Services
Building 31, Room 8A-16
Bethesda, MD 20892

Epilepsy Canada
2099 Alexandre de Seve
Suite 27
Montreal, Quebec H2L 4K8

Epilepsy Foundation of America
4351 Garden City Drive
Suite 406
Landover, MD 20785
1-800-EFA-1000

National Information Center for Children
    and Youth with Handicaps
P.O. Box 1492
Washington, DC 20013
1-800-999-5599

THINGS TO DO AND THINK ABOUT

These projects will help you learn more about people living with epilepsy.

1. People are often afraid to talk about having epilepsy because there has been so much negative information about it. If you or a friend have epilepsy, talk and share information so that you are comfortable with the subject. You will find that epilepsy has very little to do with your friendship, but talking about it will make your friendship better. Some of the things that go on inside the head of someone who is having a seizure are very interesting when you stop being afraid.

2. People with epilepsy, like people with other disabilities, are sometimes not allowed to do things for reasons that are not justified. Until recently, prejudice and ignorance allowed for laws in some places that prevented people with epilepsy from getting married. Find out more about how it feels to be overprotected and denied the right to grow by asking someone with epilepsy about this.

3. Most local chapters of the Epilepsy Foundation of America will send speakers out to talk to groups. Call and ask for a speaker to come to your class or club to tell you more about epilepsy.

4. Many people don't know anything about epilepsy except that it causes convulsions. But as you've read, there are many other types of epilepsy. Sadly, this means that some people don't know they have it — especially children. They may think that the periods of absence or confusion, the strange smells or sounds, or the odd feelings they have followed by fainting are signs of serious physical or mental illness. If you or someone you know has episodes like this, show this book to a grownup who will listen to you — a parent, grandparent, teacher, or counselor. Tell them how this affects you and ask them to help you find the right doctor to talk to about this.

GLOSSARY OF WORDS ABOUT EPILEPSY

Here are some words that will help you understand more about epilepsy and its treatment.

absence seizure: a seizure which causes a person to be briefly unconscious, usually staring straight ahead.

aura: a feeling, sense, or sign that tells a person that a seizure is going to occur. It can feel like a cool wind from inside (the most common aura) or something that only the person experiencing it will recognize as a sign. Not all people with epilepsy have auras. The word *aura* means "cool breeze."

biofeedback: a system of treatment that teaches a person how to control pain or seizures. People learn to recognize signs that something is about to occur and use their powers of concentration to head it off.

CAT scan: an image made by equipment consisting of a computer and X-ray equipment. Unlike a regular X-ray which takes only one picture, a CAT scanner can take a series of pictures. With the aid of a computer, it builds a three-dimensional impression of a part of the body.

conscious: the state of knowing what is going on around you.

convulsion: a type of seizure that causes the person to lose consciousness and fall to the ground. The person's body will first stiffen, then begin jerking movements. The movements will begin to slow down, and the person will regain consciousness, probably within a minute or two. Sometimes, but not always, there will be a loss of bladder and bowel control, a froth of saliva around the mouth, shallow breathing, and a bluish skin color. This type of seizure used to be called a "grand mal" seizure and is now often called a "tonic-clonic" seizure.

diagnosis: a doctor's determination that a person has a certain condition. In epilepsy, the diagnosis is based on what the patient says, what the doctor observes, and laboratory tests.

epilepsy: a condition that is caused by recurring and temporary overloads of electrical energy in the brain. The overload results in a variety of types of seizures, depending on where overload occurs in the brain.

generalized seizure: a seizure that occurs when the whole brain receives an overload of energy. A generalized seizure usually results in a convulsion or absence seizure.

medication: chemical treatment for an illness or condition that either cures it or, as in epilepsy, prevents or lessens symptoms such as seizures.

partial seizure: a seizure that occurs when only part of the brain receives extra energy. A partial seizure can take many forms, depending on what part of the brain is affected.

reflexes: movements or activities over which the person has little or no control. Blinking and breathing are reflexes. When a person has a seizure, the brain causes reflex actions until the extra energy stops controlling the activity.

seizure: an activity caused by an overload of electrical energy to the brain or to some part of it. There are many types of seizures, from slight finger twitches to unconsciousness. Most last no more than a minute or two; some last a few seconds. Epilepsy is a *seizure disorder*, and some people prefer to use this term.

unconscious: the state of not knowing what is going on around a person, like being asleep.

47

INDEX